SERGIO ARAGONES

MAD® MENAGERIE

WARNER BOOKS

A Warner Communications Company

WARNER BOOKS EDITION

For information address:
E.C. Publications, Inc.
485 Madison Avenue
New York, N.Y. 10022

Title "MAD" used with permission of its owner,
E.C. Publications, Inc.

This Warner Books Edition is published by
arrangement with E.C. Publications, Inc.

Warner Books, Inc.
666 Fifth Avenue
New York, N.Y. 10103

A Warner Communications Company

Printed in the United States of America

First Printing: April, 1983

Reissued: January, 1989

10 9 8 7 6 5 4 3 2

TO BENJAMIN, COLL, MINGOTE, OSKI, FOLA, ISSAC QUEZADA, VIP, BOSC, CHAVAL, FRANÇOIS, MOSE, TREZ, KOVARSKY ... FROM WHOM I LEARNED...

ATT...
CHOOO

MOM
HATE

2

3

4

5

1

2

3

4

5

1

2

3

1

2

1

2

3

4

5

6

7

8

1

2

3

5

1

2

3

1
MAIL
2
US MAIL
ARF!
ARF!
ARF!

3
ARF!
ARF!
4
ARF!
ARF!
ARF!!
ARF!

5
Grrr...
Grrr...

6
Grrr...

7
Grooooo.

8
TUMP!

1
2

3

4

5

1
$$
FOR SALE

2
FOR SALE

3
$
FOR SALE

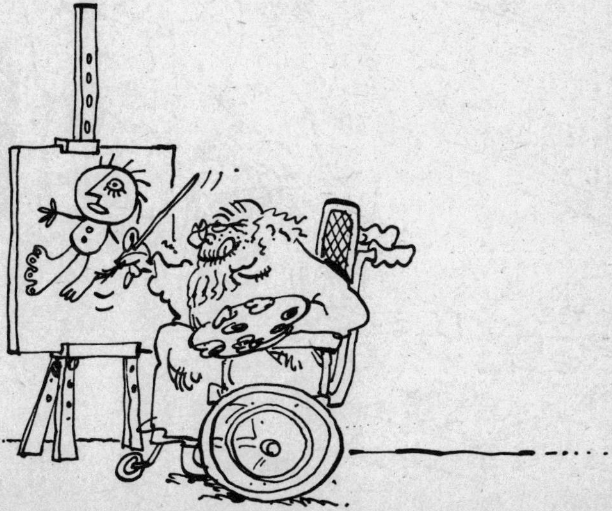

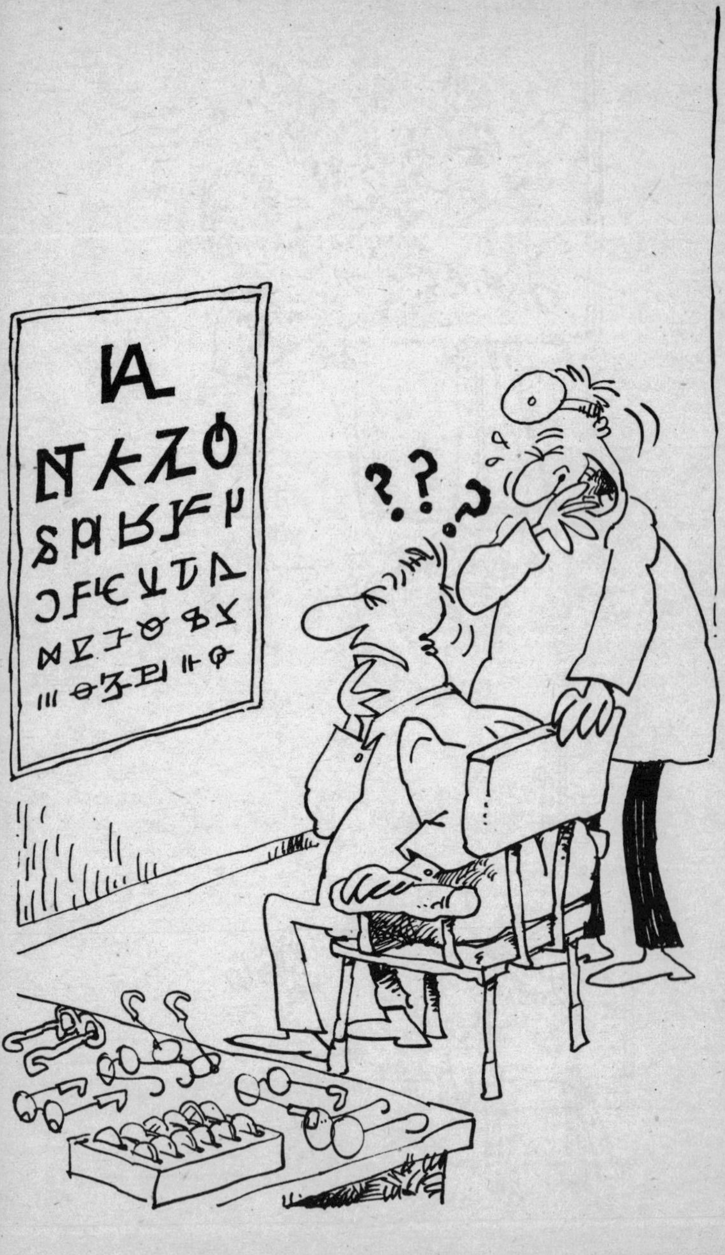

1

2

3

4

5

1

2
6

3

4

5
SCRATCH!!
SCRATCH!!

1

HOTEL
READ CROAKERS
NUDE PHOTOGRAPHY
Girls Girls
BAR
NUDE
MISS

2

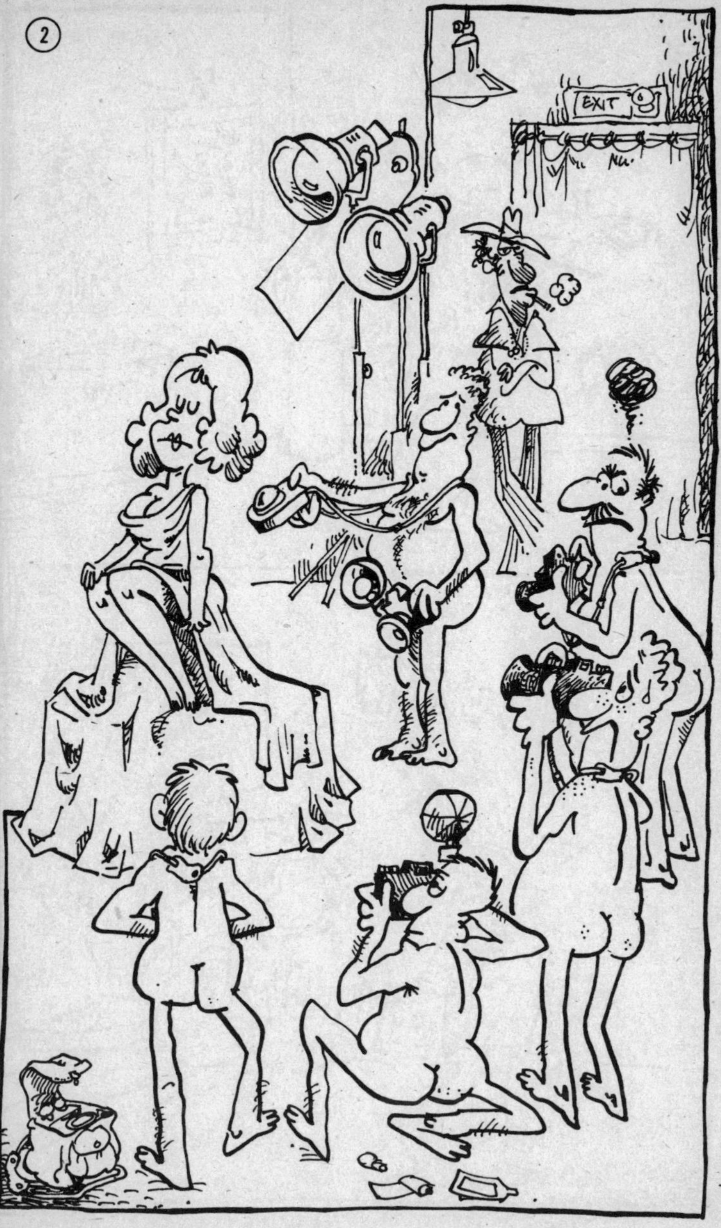

1
2
THUMP!
THUMP!
THUMP!

3
4
SHHH!
SLAM!

5
DON'T SMOKE
6

7

8
SHHH!!

1
DICK YOUNG
DREAMQUEST

2

SPECIAL EFFECTS

1
Z Z Z Z
2

③

④

5

6

1

(2)

3

4

5

6

1

2

3

2

③

4

5

1
ROCK

4

5

6
ROCK
PUNK!

①

3

1
2

3

4

5

6

1
2
3.

1

2

3
4
L.W

5

6

7

8

76

1

2

③

④

5

6

7

8

9

10

①

②

(3)

(4)

(1)

2

3

1

2

3

4
TWANGG!!

5

CACTUS
OUT OF
BUSINESS

1
MATERNITY
WARD
2
MATERNITY
WARD

3

4

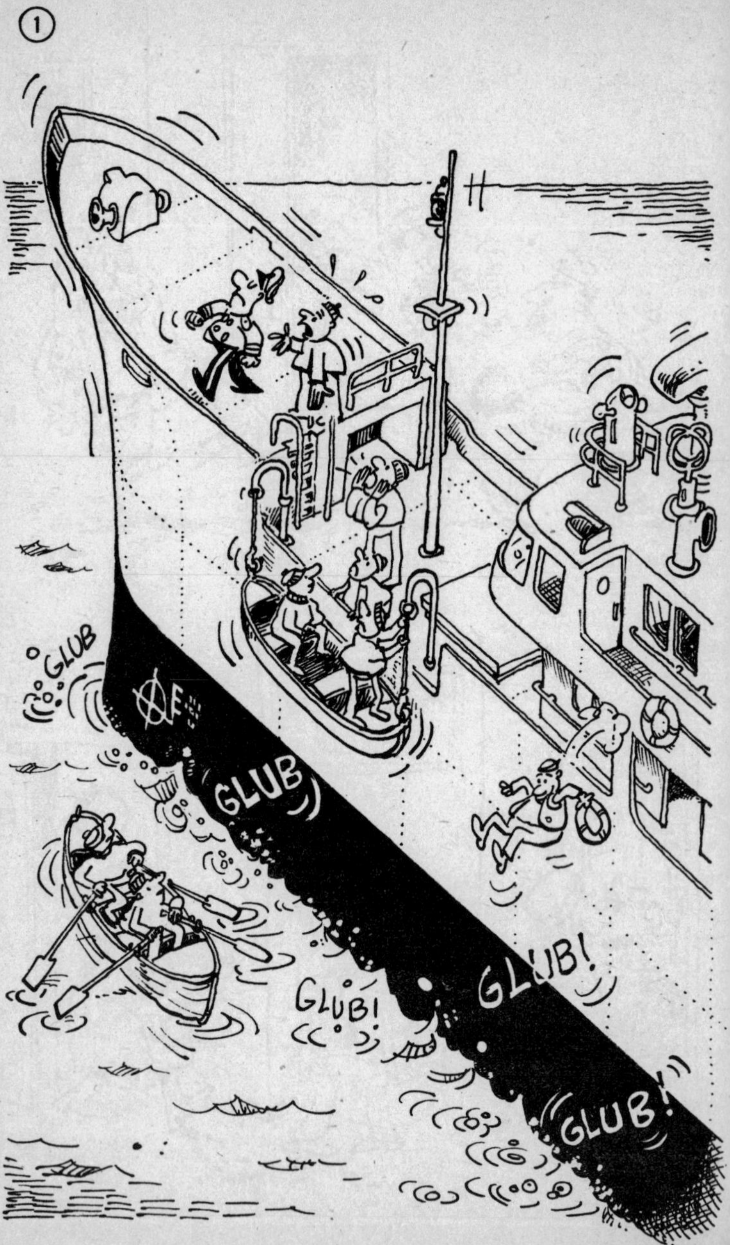
1
GLUB
GLUB
GLUB!
GLUB!
GLUB!

2
GLUB!
GLUB!
GLUB!

3

4

1

2

3

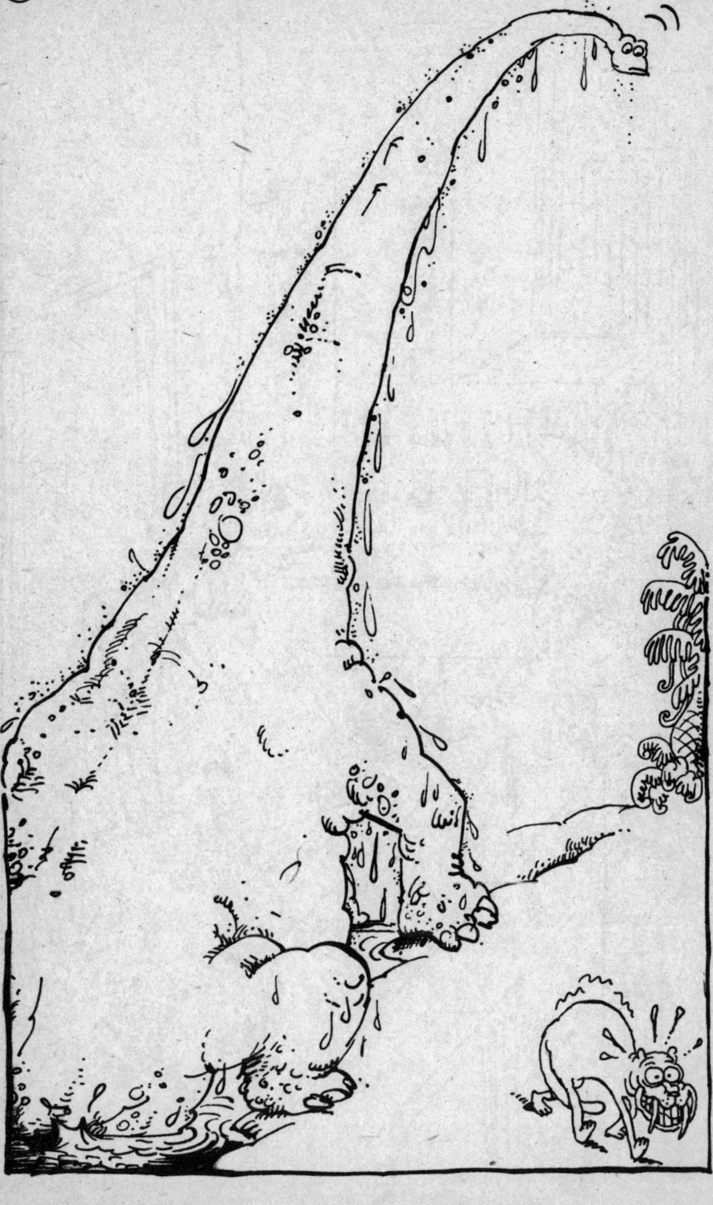

1

2

3

5

1
PIGS
2
FORELOIN
LOIN
RIBS
SHOULDER
BACON
HAM
FEET

3

4

5

1
BOARDING PASSES
PAF
2
BOARDING PASSES
PAF

3
BOARDING PASSES
PAF

1

2

3

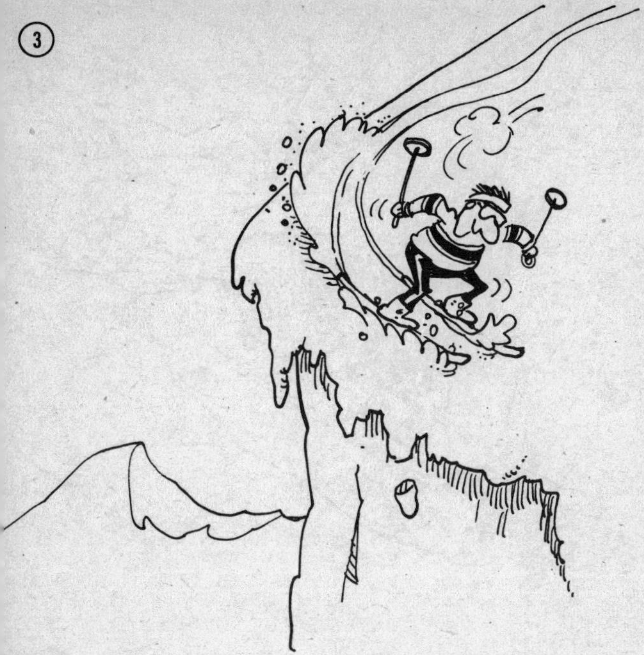

4

WOOSH!

7

8

1
2

3

4

5

1
ZOO

2

3
SLEEPING DARTS
4
THUMP!

5
ZZZZZ

6
ZZZzzz
SHAW!
MARU
FRAGIL
FRAG

7
?
TARZ
APES

TAP..
TAP..
TAP..
TAP..
TAP..

1

2

3
THWACK!

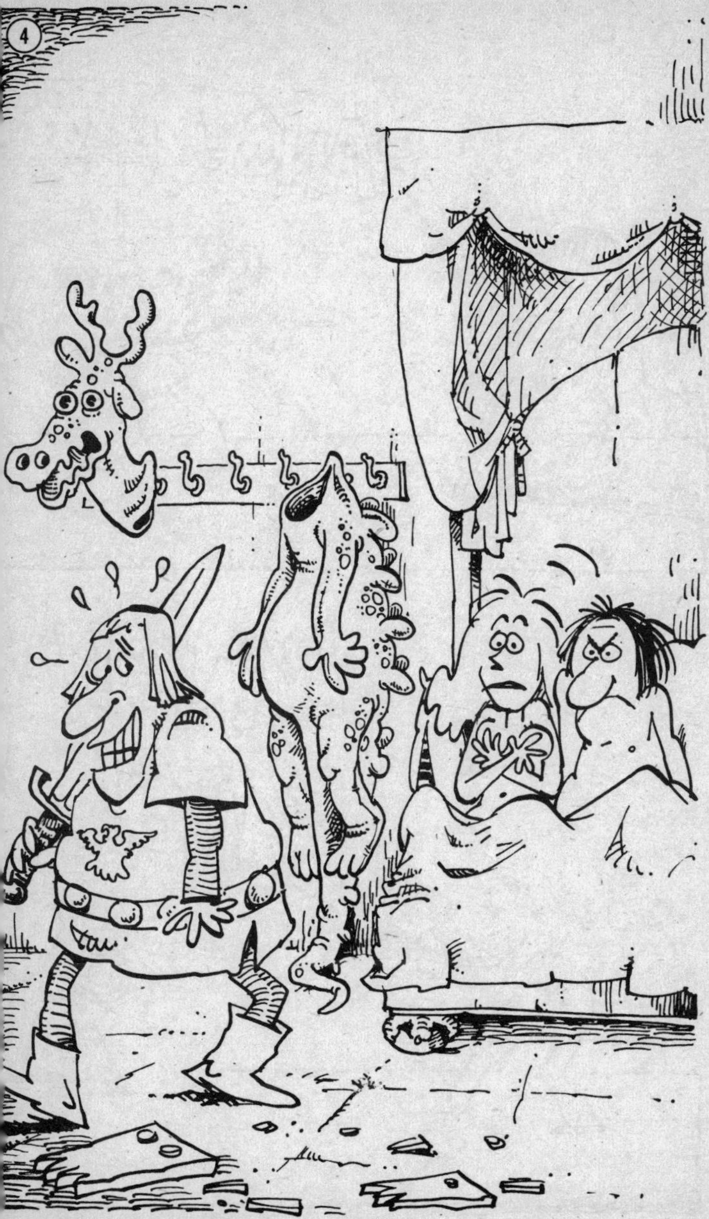
4

1
BANG!
SHOOT-
PRACTIC
2
BANG!!
BANG!

3

4

5

6

1

2

3

1

2

3

4

1

2

3

1
2

3
4

5

6

7
BAAAA
GROWLNG!
BAAAH
BAAA
BAAA

(1)

2

3

4

5

6

7

8

1
FLIGHT 40

2
FLIGHT 40
MÜNCHEN
SINGAPUR
MEXICO
LONDON
BALI

3
FLIGHT 40

①

2

3

4

1

(2)

3

THE END
...AND A FEW MORE TO ADD TO MY MAD MENAGERIE!
30-431-X, $1.95
VIVA MAD

30-425-5, $1.95

30-428-X, $1.95

30-423-9, $1.95

30-427-1, $1.95

30-424-7, $1.95
INCURABLY MAD

30-430-1, $1.95
SHOOTIN' MAD

30-429-8, $1.95
MAD MARGINALS!

30-426-3, $1.95
MAD AS A HATTER!

AND...